# You're Amazing And I'll Prove It!

My favorite part of the book was the comparing, because it was fun!
—Lisanne, age 9

The Prologue was outstanding and pulled me into the book.
—*Emma*, age 12

I loved the book. It is very informative. I don't believe that it is purely a children's book. I think it could be used in any situation with adults who have preset prejudices. I could see it used in Sunday school classes as well. This is an important message that needs to reach as many as possible.
—*Grandma D*

I learned from the book that no matter what you look like or act like, we are all really the same inside.
—Sydney, age 12

My favorite part of the book was where they explain what everything is better at/meant for.
—*Alexander,* age 10

Neal's message is a timely one. He addresses the problem of intolerance in ways that young people can understand and relate to. His real-life experiences open a discussion for readers to explore their own feelings and experiences.
—Susan Carlson, 3rd grade teacher

Sam really enjoyed the book—especially the longer stories. I was a bit surprised, in fact, because Sam is usually a kid who likes graphic novels, so I didn't know what he would think. He was particularly intrigued by the stories involving basketball!
—*Heidi,* Sam's mom

# Read the Prologue and you will be HOOKED!

# You're Amazing
## And I'll Prove It!

# Neal G. Brownell

## Illustrated by
## Rich Molinelli

Knowledge Is Freedom
Publishing

Manufactured in the United States of America

First Printing: 2018

Knowledge Is Freedom Publishing
702 Acorn Hill Road
Olivebridge, NY  12461

Illustrations and book cover by Rich Molinelli
*www.richmolinelli.com*

Book cover design, interior design by Joe Tantillo
*tantillo.artwork@gmail.com*

Editing and mentoring by Susan Uttendorfsky
*www.adirondackediting.com*

ISBN # 978-0-9998376-1-0
Library of Congress Control Number 2018913523

# Dedication & Acknowledgments

I want to thank all of the amazing people whose influence helped me with this book. Starting with my late wife, Debra C. Kading Brownell (Deb, aka Hunskybunsky). Without your love, compassion, and tenacity, I would not even be here. I miss you. I didn't give you permission to die, but I know for a fact I will see you again.

To my wife, Linda Mae Wilson Brownell (Linda, aka Sweetiebeetie), whom I not only love with every fiber of my being, I also like every ounce of who you are. I look forward to waking up and spending my days with you. I thank your mom, Esther, for sending you to me. This book would not have happened without the love and joy you bring to my life.

To my best friend Dave Lewis: Thank you for taking the time to put the final pieces in place. These final pieces allowed me to become who I am.

To Helen Fleming, who, at the ripe old age of 12/13, did all of the preliminary drawings for this book. Without your help, I would not have been able to finish this book. It was a joy and a pleasure to work with someone so gifted. We look forward to seeing great things from you in the future.

Last, but not least, I want to thank everyone I have ever known. All of you have influenced my life in such amazing and awe-inspiring ways. Because of you, I see the world as the incredible, wondrous place it is meant to be.

# Table of Contents

# PROLOGUE

## Doorway to Knowledge & Freedom

**Open for Business**

# Prologue

*Q**uestion: How do you tell someone that everyone is special and then get them to internalize, understand, believe, and then act on this new knowledge?***

*A**nswer:* You don't tell the person—you have to show them. You have to get the person engaged by asking questions. Questions like, "Who's better? Is a brightly colored bird better than a dull plain brown bird?" You then show the two birds sitting on a nest with eggs in it and ask the same questions again. Once you've had the person answer, you show them that both birds are from the same family. One is a male and one is a female and the two birds are equally important to the survival of the babies. This is just one of many questions *You're Amazing And I'll Prove It!* asks to show the reader how everything and everyone has special attributes that make them unique and exceptionally important.

Entwined with the questions, *You're Amazing And I'll Prove It!* has real-life stories about seemingly unremarkable people doing extraordinary things. *You're Amazing And I'll Prove It!* shows the reader how each and every one of us has extraordinary gifts given to us at birth.

Knowledge and acceptance of oneself, as well as others, is freedom. *You're Amazing And I'll Prove It!* engages readers to the point where they internalize, understand, and believe—and then are able to act on the knowledge that all people are exceptionally special. It shows that, regardless of race, age, gender, religion, or any other difference you can find, by accepting others, we are giving freedom not only to the people around us, but also to ourselves.

A s you look around our amazing world, you see a myriad of things that are made by both Mother Nature and by man. You see animals, plants and insects, as well as lamps, tables, planes, helicopters, and ships. Most of these animals, plants, insects, planes, and helicopters come in different sizes, colors, and shapes. Although each of these things is similar in some ways, they are very different in others. For instance, let's say you have two dogs—one of them is a large Great Dane and the other is a Chihuahua. They are both dogs, and that makes them the same. However, one is big and the other is small, which makes them different.

In the first part of this book, we are going to look at and compare eight different groupings. Each one of the animals, plants, or man-made objects will have a similar animal, plant, or man-made object next to it. All I want you to do is compare the two objects. Once you have looked at the two objects, I want you to answer one simple question: "Is object A better than object B, or is B better than A?"

In the next part of this book, we will look at the same things and discuss why you answered the way you did.

Before we get started, I want to take a moment to congratulate you on being an exceptionally special person. I already know you are an extraordinary person, whether you know you are or not. Keep reading and I will prove it to you.

Now we can get started. Turn the page.

# Room 1

## Let's Compare

Welcome

# Which one of these trees is better?

| *Tall, Full, Green Leafy Tree* | *Short, Scrawny, Scraggly Tree* |
| --- | --- |

Which one of these trees is better? Do you think the tall, full, green leafy tree is better than the short, scrawny, scraggly tree?

On the other hand, do you think the short, scrawny, scraggly tree is better than the tall, full, green leafy tree?

# Which one of these cats do you think is better?

*Fluffy Persian Cat*

*Cat With No Hair*

**W**hich cat do you think is better? Do you think the fluffy Persian cat is better than the cat with no hair?

Alternatively, do you think the cat with no hair is better than the fluffy Persian cat?

# Which one of these dogs do you think is better?

*Dog With The Wrinkled Face* | *Powerful, Athletic, Playful Dog*

Which one of these dogs do you think is better? Is the dog with the wrinkled face that slobbers all over itself better than the powerful, athletic, playful dog?

Then again, is the powerful, athletic, playful dog better than the dog with the wrinkled face that slobbers all over itself?

# Which of these women is taking care of herself?

*Woman Sitting In A Chair*

*Woman Who's Exercising*

Which of these women is taking care of herself? Is the woman sitting in a chair doing nothing taking care of herself?

Then again, is the woman who's exercising taking care of herself? Is one of the women better than the other because she is taking care of herself?

# Which of these spiders do you think is better?

| Big, Strong Spider | Small, Fragile Spider |

Which one of these spiders do you think is better? Is the big, strong spider better than the small, fragile spider?

In contrast, is the small, fragile spider better than the big, strong spider?

# Is a small cat better than a big German Shepherd?

*Small Cat*

*Big German Shepherd*

Is a small cat better than a big German Shepherd?

On the other hand, is a big German Shepherd better than a small cat?

# Which bird do you think is better than the other?

| Big, Powerful Eagle | Small, Delicate Hummingbird |

Which bird do you think is better than the other? Is the big, powerful eagle better than the small, delicate hummingbird?

In contrast, is the small, delicate hummingbird better than the big, powerful eagle?

# Is the small ship better than the big ship?

| *Small Ship With 3 Cannons* | *Big Ship With 30 Cannons* |

Which one of these ships is better? Is the small ship with 3 cannons better than the big ship with 30 cannons?

Then again, is the big ship with 30 cannons better than the small ship with 3 cannons?

# ROOM 2

## Does It Make a Difference?

**Come In & Decide**

Now that you have looked at, thought about, and decided who or what is better on each of the last eight pages, let's take a closer look. However, this time let's add some more information. I want you to take another look at each of the comparisons. Decide if the setting they are in changes your original answer—or does your original answer remain the same?

# Which one did you choose?

| *Tall, Full, Green Leafy Tree* | *Short, Scrawny, Scraggly Tree* |

When I showed you these two trees, which one did you choose as the better one? Did you choose the tall, full, green leafy tree? On the other hand, did you choose the short, scrawny, scraggly tree?

# Drawing 1A

Tall, Full, Green Leafy Tree

Short, Scrawny, Scraggly Tree

Take another look. If the trees are located at the bottom of a mountain, with lots of tall trees around them (Drawing 1A), do you want to change your original answer?

# Drawing 1B

Tall, Full, Green Leafy Tree

Short, Scrawny, Scraggly Tree

Now look at the exact same two trees. If the trees are located on top of a mountain, with few or no other trees around them (Drawing 1B), which tree do you think is better? Do these conditions change your original answer?

The answer to these questions came to me one day when some friends and I hiked to the top of a mountain. When we started at the bottom of the mountain, the

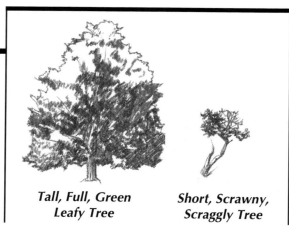

**Tall, Full, Green Leafy Tree**   **Short, Scrawny, Scraggly Tree**

trees were tall and robust. However, as we climbed the mountain, the trees got shorter and stouter. After reaching the peak of this mountain, I noticed all the trees were very short and haggard, but very stout looking. That was when I asked myself which tree was better: The tall, full, green leafy tree or the short, scrawny, scraggly tree?

After thinking about it, I realized that if you take the two trees and put them at the bottom of a mountain, then the tall tree is better than the short tree. This is because the tall tree will get all the sunlight, however the short tree will get no sunlight and die.

However, if you take the same two trees and put them at the top of the mountain, the short tree is better than the tall one. Why, you may ask? The answer is that at the top of the mountain, there is lots and lots of wind and the weather is much harsher than at the bottom. At the top of the mountain, the wind is too strong and ferocious for the tall tree. The tall tree would be blown down and die. However, the short tree has much less surface area for the wind to blow against. So under these circumstances, not only can the short tree survive, it can thrive. With these advantages over the tall tree, the short tree is the better tree at the top of a mountain.

# Which one did you choose?

*Fluffy Persian Cat*

*Cat With No Hair*

Next, I asked you to take a look at these two cats and decide which one is better. Did you choose the fluffy Persian cat as the better cat, or did you choose the cat with no hair?

Now I want you to look at these two cats in different situations.

## Drawing 2A

In the first situation (Drawing 2A), the two cats are outside on a cold winter day. Does your original answer as to which cat is better remain the same?

# Drawing 2B

In the second situation (Drawing 2B), both cats are inside a warm home, sitting on the bed of a person who is allergic to cats. Does your original answer change?

**Drawing 2A**          **Drawing 2B**

The answer to the question "Which cat is better?" depends on the situation. It is pretty obvious what the strengths of the cat with hair are. Hair keeps the cat warm on cold days. It also provides camouflage from predators. So the cat with hair is better when it is outside on a cold day.

But what advantages could a cat with no hair have? There are many people who love cats but are allergic to cat hair. Although the Sphynx, a type of hairless cat, is not hypoallergenic, it can make a perfect pet for people who love cats but have allergies. For them, the hairless cat is better than the cat with hair.

# Which one did you choose?

*Dog With The Wrinkled Face* | *Powerful, Athletic, Playful Dog*

In the third set of drawings, I asked you to look at and compare these two dogs. When you looked at the two dogs, which one did you pick as the better dog? Did you pick the dog with the wrinkled face that slobbers all over itself, or did you pick the powerful, athletic, playful dog?

# Drawing 3A

Take a look at the situations in Drawings 3A and 3B. Imagine that a three-year-old girl is lost and the police need help finding her.

# Drawing 3B

If you had to decide which dog was going to help the police find the little girl, which dog would you decide was better? Would you pick the dog with the wrinkled face that slobbers all over itself? Then again, would you pick the powerful, athletic, playful dog?

## Drawing 3C

Now take a look at the situations in Drawings 3C and 3D. In this situation, imagine you need a dog to watch over and take care of a baby. If this was the case, which dog would you pick as the better dog?

# Drawing 3D

Would you pick the dog with the wrinkled face that slobbers all over itself, or would you pick the powerful, athletic, playful dog?

Has your original answer changed after seeing these two remarkably different dogs in these diverse situations?

*Dog With The Wrinkled Face*     *Powerful, Athletic, Playful Dog*

With these comparisons, the answer to which dog is better depends on what you need the dog to do. These dogs are both in a class called the "working dogs" class. Like all working dogs, they are specifically adapted to their specialties.

The dog with the wrinkled face that slobbers all over itself is a Bloodhound.[1] All dogs have the ability to smell much better than humans. However, the Bloodhound's ability to track a person or another animal is absolutely amazing. The Bloodhound is the number one breed used for tracking. It has wrinkly skin with lots of folds all over its face and neck. It has large, long, floppy ears and slobbers a lot.

These traits are what make Bloodhounds so special for tracking. All the folds and wrinkly skin, along with their slobbering, helps them trap the microscopic scent particles they are tracking. Their large, floppy ears also help to guide the scent particles to their nose. So, if you need a dog who can help the police find a lost little girl—as in Drawings 3A and 3B—the better dog by far is the Bloodhound. Later in this book, I have a story about a Bloodhound named Yogi. This story emphasizes just how extraordinary Bloodhounds are.

This brings us back to the question asked in Drawings 3C and 3D. Which dog is the better dog if you need a dog to watch over and take care of a baby? The answer is you need the gentle, playful, loyal, fearless dog with the maternal instinct. This dog is the American Pit Bull.[2] That's right, you need the very dog that uneducated people are trying to tell you is so dangerous.

30

Nowadays, this dog's breed has a lot of misconceptions tied to it. However, the misconceptions are just that—misconceptions. The truth is that this breed is amazingly gentle, friendly, playful, and full of energy. It is known for being extremely strong, very fast, and absolutely tenacious. This dog simply will not give up. You would think this would be enough traits for any breed. However, this breed is also known for being astonishingly loyal and completely fearless in the face of danger. Oh, and this breed has one more extremely important trait. It has an incredibly strong maternal instinct. This maternal, gentle instinct, along with its instinct to protect, is the reason this dog has been used for more than 100 years to watch over, play with, and protect children. I have a story about Mercy, an American Pit Bull, later in this book. In this story I show you how I learned that American Pit Bulls are absolutely incredible animals.

# Which one did you choose?

*Woman Sitting In A Chair*

*Woman Who's Exercising*

When I had you look at these two women, I asked you which one was taking care of herself. Which woman did you choose: The woman exercising or the woman sitting in the chair?

## Drawing 4A     ## Drawing 4B

*Woman Sitting In A Chair*

*Woman Who's Exercising*

*Woman Sleeping*

*Woman Exhausted*

When you look at the women in these two drawings (Drawing 4A and Drawing 4B), does your original answer change?

**Woman Sitting In
A Chair**

**Woman Who's
Exercising**

As with the previous drawings you have looked at, the question about which woman is taking care of herself cannot be answered without you having more information. The information you need in this case is how a person's body builds muscle. You also need to know how the body heals itself in order to stay healthy. When a person is exercising, they are actually breaking down their muscles. As they exercise, the muscles are getting more and more tired until they can't exercise any more. This breaking down of the muscles tells the body that it needs to get stronger in order for it to perform better.

However, after breaking the muscles down by exercising, the body needs to rebuild itself with stronger, more resilient muscles. The body does this rebuilding during times of rest. When the body is resting or sleeping, it is working hard to become stronger. This way the body can do more strenuous exercising next time.

As you can see, the answer to which woman is taking care of herself can be either one, both of them, or neither.

If the answer is that neither one is taking care of herself, this would mean that the woman who is exercising isn't getting enough rest for her body to strengthen itself. Without enough rest, her body actually becomes weaker. At the same time, if the woman who is resting isn't getting enough exercise, then her body doesn't strengthen itself. In this case, her body also becomes weaker.

Perhaps you have answered that both women are taking care

of themselves. This would mean that both women are exercising enough to let their bodies know they need to strengthen themselves. At the same time, both women are getting enough rest to allow their bodies the time they need to strengthen themselves.

# Which one did you choose?

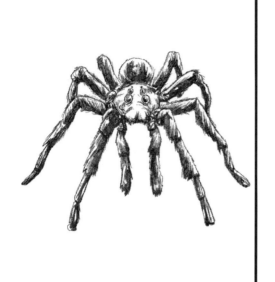

*Big, Strong Spider* | *Small, Fragile Spider*

Which spider did you pick as the better one? Do you think it is pretty obvious the big, strong spider is the better spider? In contrast, did you find something in the small, fragile spider that makes you think it's better?

Regardless of which spider you picked, let's see if your answer changes after we look at both of them in two different situations.

# Drawing 5A

Big, Strong Spider

Small, Fragile Spider

A s you can see in Drawing 5A, the two spiders are now in a brightly lit room. In this situation, is one spider better than the other? Does this situation change your original answer?

Once more, regardless of what your answer is, take a look at the same two spiders in this next situation.

# Drawing 5B

Big, Strong Spider

Small, Fragile Spider

Unlike the situations in our previous comparisons, the situation depicted in Drawing 5B may not seem very different from the situation in Drawing 5A. If you compare the two drawings, you will notice they are drawings of the same room. The only difference is that in Drawing 5B, the drapes are pulled, which makes the room dark. Although there is almost no variation between the two situations, does this slight dissimilarity make any difference in your original answer?

# Does It Make A Difference?

Although the only deviation between the two drawings is the amount of light filtering through the windows, this makes a massive impact on which spider is better. You are probably asking yourself why this slight deviation makes such a massive difference. The answer to your question came to me one day while my wife Linda and I were cleaning. Linda and I have a house cleaning business. One day while cleaning a brightly lit room, I noticed there was a really big spider in one of the corners. I went ahead and vacuumed up the spider, then went back to cleaning the room. After finishing the cleaning of that room, I went into the very next room to clean it. This room was a guest bedroom. It was almost never used. The window shades were pulled down. With the exception of a tiny amount of light that came in around the shades, the room was dark the vast majority of the time.

While cleaning this room, I noticed a small spider by the window. I asked myself, "Why a big spider in a brightly lit room and a small spider in a dark room?" After thinking about it for a little while, I realized the reason the big, strong spider was in the brightly lit room was that lots of insects were drawn to the light. That meant there was lots of food for the big, strong spider to eat.

However, in the dark room, there was only a fraction of that light to draw insects. A tiny amount of light meant almost no insects. Almost no insects meant very little food for spiders. With such little amounts of food, the big, strong spider could not survive there. Although the big, strong spider would perish in the dark room, the small, fragile spider had plenty of food to thrive. This means that in the dark room, the small, fragile spider is far better than the big, strong spider.

The next question I asked was if the small, fragile spider has enough food in both the dark room and the bright room, why would it not be better in both rooms? The answer to this question is that in the bright room the small, fragile spider might not survive—the big, strong spider could eat the small, fragile spider.

So, which spider is better? The answer is two-fold. In the brightly lit room, the big, strong spider is better. In the dark room, the small, fragile spider is better.

# Which one did you choose?

*Small Cat*

*Big German Shepherd*

**W**as it difficult deciding whether the small cat or the big German Shepherd dog was better?

Regardless of whether you picked the dog or the cat, let's put the two of them in a few different circumstances and see if your answer changes or remains the same.

## Drawing 6A

Take a look at Drawing 6A. Who do you think is better? In this situation, you are living in a tiny apartment. Do you think a small cat or a big German Shepherd would be the most desirable pet? In other words, which is the better pet in this situation?

## Drawing 6B

## Drawing 6C

*Seeing Eye Dog*

*Seeing Eye Cat*

When you look at Drawings 6B and 6C, which pet is better in this situation? As you can see, the man in the drawings is blind. Which pet would be most advantageous for the blind man to own? Would you pick a Seeing Eye dog over a cat? On the other hand, would you pick a Seeing Eye cat over a dog?

## Drawing 6D

In Drawing 6D, imagine you live in an extremely large house. However, you are away on business trips for two or three days at a time. This means that you need a pet that can fend for itself while you are away. In this case, which pet is better? Would you pick the small cat or the big German Shepherd to be left alone for two or three days at a time?

# Drawing 6E

In the fourth scenario, you are living in a high crime area. You are home alone when someone breaks in (Drawing 6E). Would you want a small cat to help protect you, or would you pick the big German Shepherd?

*Small Cat*        *Big German Shepherd*

**B**y now, you have learned it really depends on the situation the animals are in, in order to determine whether one is better than the other. As far as house pets go, cats are more independent than dogs. As long as there is food, water, and a litter box, cats can be left unattended for two or three days. Dogs can only be left alone for eight to ten hours. House cats are also small and are all about the same size, but dogs vary in size. So if you need a pet that is small and can be left at home while you are away from home for a few days, the cat is better than the dog. Therefore, in the situations depicted in Drawings 6A and 6D, the cat is the better pet.

On the other hand, although cats can be trained to do a few things, dogs can be trained for many tasks. They can be trained to do something as simple as playing fetch, or as advanced as guarding your home. There are a wide variety of dog breeds, from tiny ones to big ones the size of small horses. Dogs also have a wide variety of personalities and are extremely loyal. If you need a pet that can be trained specifically for you or your needs, the dog is better than the cat. This means in the situations presented in Drawings 6B, 6C, and 6E, the dog is the better pet.

# Which one did you choose?

| Big, Powerful Eagle | Small, Delicate Hummingbird |

When you looked at the eagle and the hummingbird, you probably said to yourself, "The eagle is far better." But like all the other comparisons, let's put these two birds in a specific scenario.

# Drawing 7A

| *Big, Powerful Eagle* | *Small, Delicate Hummingbird* |

Take a look at Drawing 7A. As you can see, this Bald Eagle is swooping down on the hummingbird. In this scenario, is the big, powerful Bald Eagle better than the small, delicate hummingbird? We need to look at both the strengths and weaknesses of both birds in order to answer the question.

L et's start with the Bald Eagle. What are some of the strengths and/or weaknesses of the Bald Eagle? They can fly straight ahead, climb in the air, or swoop down. They have an amazingly acute sense of sight. Bald Eagles can see a single fish below the water from 200 feet away. Bald Eagles are one of the largest birds of prey in the world. Their wingspan can be as much as seven feet from wing tip to wing tip. Bald Eagles attack their prey by swooping down at an angle. They can reach speeds of up to 100

mph. For their massive size, Bald Eagles can also switch directions quite rapidly. These are extraordinary abilities. Do these abilities make the Bald Eagle the better bird in the scenario presented in Drawing 7A? In order to answer this question, we need to take a closer look at the hummingbird.

What are the strengths and/or weaknesses of the hummingbird? The hummingbird is the smallest bird in the world. Most only measure about 3 to 5 inches in size. Due to the fact that they are so small, hummingbirds can flap their wings about 70 times per second in normal flight. However,

in a high-speed dive, they can flap their wings about 200 times per second. These tiny birds are the only birds in the world that can fly both forward and backward. They can hover in mid-air like a helicopter. They can fly sideways. They can even fly upside down. Hummingbirds can stop on a dime and hover. They can also change directions in a split second, and move in virtually any direction.

Like the Bald Eagle, the abilities of the hummingbird are extraordinary. However, do these abilities help or hurt a 5-inch hummingbird's chances to survive a 7-foot Bald Eagle swooping down at 100 mph? What do you think?

The answer to the question, which bird is better, is that until the Bald Eagle actually has the hummingbird in its claws, the hummingbird's abilities to move in any direction in a fraction of a second absolutely gives it an extremely good chance to get away. This is because, the very thing that is an advantage to either one of these birds, can also be a disadvantage.

Therefore, in the scenario depicted in Drawing 7A on page 48, depending on each bird's split-second decisions, either the Bald Eagle or the hummingbird could be the better bird.

# Which one did you choose?

| Small Ship With 3 Cannons | Big Ship With 30 Cannons |

In the final drawings of Room 1, I asked you to decide which ship is better. After looking a second time at the first seven comparisons, I bet you think you already know the answer! Why don't we save the comparing of the small ship with the big ship for a bit later in this book.

# ROOM 3

## More Alike Than Different

## Are There any Differences?

---

In this room, let's compare photos of the human body. For the next few photos, I am going to ask you if you can see any differences between the photos. The only things I may have changed from the originals are the actual sizes. I have made them all the same size, so you can compare the photos more easily.

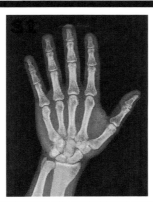

**S1**

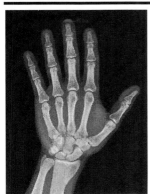

**S2**

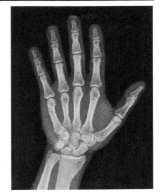

**S3**

Take a look at these three skeletal hands. Do you see any differences between them?

You shouldn't spend a lot of time looking. Just spend a moment or two. Ask yourself, "Are the fingertips all the same?" Are each of the fingers, from the thumb to the little finger, the same? Look at the wrist area of each hand. Are there any variations in any of the bones?

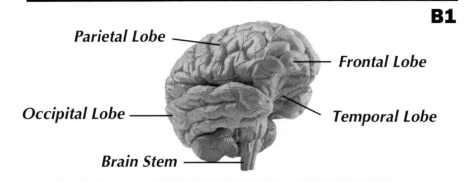

**B1**

Parietal Lobe

Frontal Lobe

Occipital Lobe

Temporal Lobe

Brain Stem

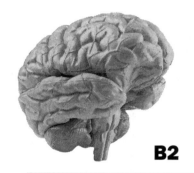

**B2**

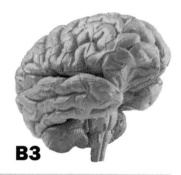

**B3**

A s you can see, on this page there are three brains. Like the skeletal hands on the last page, I want you to take a quick look. Do you see any differences, or are they the same? Again, like the skeletal hands, don't spend a lot of time. Just take a moment and isolate different parts of each brain. First, look at the frontal lobe of brain B1 and compare it with the frontal lobe of brain B2 and brain B3. If you don't see any variation in any of the frontal lobes, move on to other sections of each brain.

Now let's move on to the last set of photos in this section.

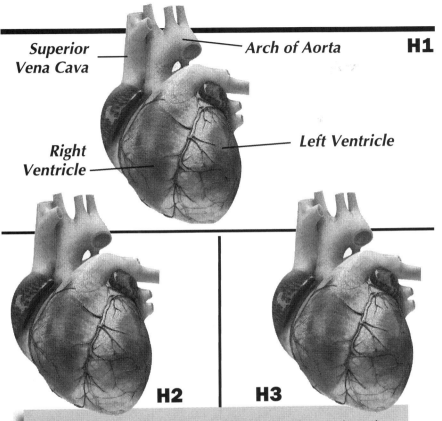

Superior Vena Cava

Arch of Aorta

**H1**

Right Ventricle

Left Ventricle

**H2**

**H3**

I have deliberately made these hearts larger than the skeletal hands and the brains to make them easier for you to compare. Like the last two comparisons, just spend a moment or two and compare these three hearts. Are these hearts all the same, or are there some differences? As you can see, I have named a few of the parts. This should also make it easier for you to examine the different parts.

Regardless of whether you answer they are all the same or you think there are some differences, for now, let's move on to the next section. We will revisit the skeletal hands, the brains, and the hearts later in this book.

# Room 4

## Which Person is Better?

Keep Thinking

If you were dealing with three people from different parts of the world that have diverse shades of color in their skin, who would you think is better: An Asian lawyer, a black doctor, or a white short person with no formal schooling? As you have seen in the previous pages of this book, you can't answer this question without knowing the situation in which the three individuals find themselves.

Let's say you broke your leg. With your broken leg, which person would be the better person? Would the Asian lawyer, the black doctor, or the white short person be the better one? Obviously, if you have a broken leg, the doctor is the only one who can help you. This means that in the case of you having a broken leg, the black doctor is better than the others.

Now, let's say you have been accused of a crime that you didn't commit. You need someone to help prove your innocence. Which person is better in this case? Again, the obvious answer is that if you need legal help, the better person is the Asian lawyer.

Now that we have seen the doctor and the lawyer being better in situations that only they can help with, let's ask another question. Let's say you are lost in the wilderness and you have no idea what to do for food or shelter. You have no idea how to survive in the wilderness. Which person would be the better person—the Asian lawyer, the black doctor, or the white short person?

You are probably saying to yourself, "I can't answer that question. I don't know enough about the three people to answer." Congratulations! You have discovered that there is no such thing as one person or one thing being better than another person or thing. The only way anyone or anything is better than another is when they are placed in a specific situation and their special abilities are needed.

Now let's ask the same question again. Only this time, you will have more information to form your answer.

You are lost in the wilderness and you have no idea of what to do for food or shelter. You have no idea how to survive in the wilderness. The only people with you are an Asian lawyer, a black doctor, and a white short person with no formal schooling. However, the white short person grew up in a family that lived far away from any city. This person's parents taught them many skills, including survival skills. Among these survival skills were to know how to find food, water, and shelter. Therefore, they know everything they need to survive in the wilderness. Now I ask you again, which person is the better one: The Asian lawyer, the black doctor, or the white short person with no formal schooling? The answer to this question is also obvious; the better person in this scenario is the white short person.

Let's go even further to find out who is better. First, let's say you are on a plane with many other people. Although you don't

know it, among all these people there is an Asian lawyer and a black doctor. Suddenly, the plane starts having trouble. The pilots are unable to regain control, so the plane crashes in the wilderness. You, the black doctor, and the Asian lawyer are the only ones who survive the crash. In the crash, you break your leg and sustain some other life-threatening injuries. If you don't have help, you will die. The three of you are trapped in the wilderness. You, the black doctor, and the Asian lawyer have no idea how to survive in the wilderness.

The scene of the plane crash around you is chaotic. Suddenly, one of the local natives steps into view. Apparently, this person saw your plane crash and came to help. This local is a white short person who knows how to survive in the wilderness. This person has lived all their life in the wilderness. Although they know how to survive in the wilderness, the white short person has no idea how to signal for help.

Even though you don't know how to survive in the wilderness, you do know how to signal for help. Once you are able to, you show the others how to signal for help and you are rescued. Now that you are rescued, you think your troubles are over. Then, suddenly, you are arrested and accused of causing the plane accident that killed all those people and left you, the Asian lawyer, and the black doctor stranded in the wilderness.

The question that needs to be answered in this scenario is: Which one of you is the best person? Is the black doctor the best? Is the white short person the best? Is the Asian lawyer the best? On the other hand, are you better than the others?

The black doctor can help with your broken leg. The white short person can show you how to survive until you are rescued. You can show everyone else how to signal for help so all of you can be rescued, and the Asian lawyer will help prove you are innocent of causing the plane crash.

In the case of the plane crash, is there any way all of you would survive until the three of you were rescued and then have you proven innocent without the expertise of the others? I ask you again—which one of you is the better person?

*You*

# What Have We Learned From These Stories?

As with virtually all the situations you will ever find yourself in, the above situation shows that you always have a choice. The two choices you have with the Asian lawyer, the black doctor, and the white short person are:

*Choice one:* You can choose narrow-minded intolerance and judge the people around you by their race, as well as other physical characteristics. If you make this choice, it could result in your death.

*Choice two:* Accept the people around you as special and unique. Work together with love and understanding toward one another. This will allow you and the others to not only survive, but also in the long run, thrive. Oh, and with choice two, you can also judge the others by their race. After all, you, the Asian lawyer, the black doctor, and the white short person are all the same race. What race do you think I'm talking about? The race you all belong to is the HUMAN RACE.

For those of you who don't know what some of these words mean, I have listed the Merriam-Webster Dictionary definitions below:

**Accept** is "to receive willingly; to give admittance or approval; to recognize as true; to make a favorable response to."

**Special** is "being unusual and especially better in some way; different from others of the same kind—unique; designed for a certain purpose."

**Bigotry** is "intolerance."

A **bigot** is "one who is strongly partial to one's own group, religion, race, or politics and is intolerant of those who differ."

An **intolerant** person is "not willing to allow some people to have equality, freedom, or other social rights."

**Narrow-minded** is when a person is "not willing to accept opinions, beliefs, or behaviors that are unusual or different from their own."

# ROOM 5

## Real Life *You're Amazing*

This is Awesome

I n three of the first four rooms, we looked at different things, animals, and people. We have seen the very thing that is an advantage in one situation can be a disadvantage in another. We also have seen that when the advantages of one thing, animal, or person are used in connection with the advantages of another's, extraordinary things can happen.

In this next section, let's look at real-life experiences. These situations show that not only can advantages be used to achieve extraordinary things, but perceived disadvantages can actually be an advantage. They also show how judging someone by their disadvantages can hurt the person who is doing the judging.

## What I Learned From a Game

# *Unexpected Hero!*

When I was growing up, I tried out for different sports. I tried baseball and was pretty good at it. However, because my family moved to different parts of the country every few years, I was always the new kid. The other kids ridiculed me all the time. Even though I was pretty good at baseball, with all the ridicule, I quit the team.

I then tried other sports and ran into the same new-kid-on-the-block ridiculing. I would join and then quit. Out of all the sports—baseball, football, etc.—basketball was my least favorite. In fact, I hated basketball. One day when I was in fifth grade, my school announced there was going to be an in-school basketball league. They also told us all we had to do was show up at practice and we would automatically be put on a team. For some unknown reason, I decided I was going to try playing this game I hated.

When I showed up, I was placed on a team named the Blazers. They told me to go shoot around. I was terrible. Not only did I not know any of the rules, I didn't even know the positions the players played on the court. When I was told I was going to play the forward position, I asked them, "What is a forward?" The coach, as well as all the kids on the team, laughed at me. They told me I was dumb for not knowing what a forward was. It was obvious I had no knowledge of the game or any natural talent for basketball.

The ridicule started immediately. They called me every hurtful name you could think of.

There were only two rules every team had to follow. The first rule was no one could be kicked off a team. The second rule was

# What I Learned From a Game

every kid on the team had to play in every game. So that meant they could not get rid of me, and they had to let me play in every game. Right in front of me, they told me I was so bad that they could never win with me on the team.

That night, I went home and cried. I wanted so badly to quit. I then took a good look at myself. I had quit everything I joined because it was hard dealing with all the ridicule. I told myself, "Neal, if you quit this, you'll be a quitter all your life." Through my tears, I told myself I was going to hang in there for the entire season no matter what.

The next day, I forced myself to go to practice. To this day, I don't know how my team did it, but they were able to trade me to another team. They told me, "We got rid of you. We don't want you on our team. Now that you are gone, we will be a winning team!" You can imagine how that made me feel.

My new team was called the Suns. When I went to the practice for my new team, they were just as belittling.

The coach introduced me to the team by saying, "Look who we have to have on our team. Now we will never win." I started crying right in front of them, but I didn't quit. I was going to stick with it all the way to the end of the season.

I went home and put a hoop up on the side of my clubhouse and started practicing. My clubhouse was just a little playhouse my little brother and

# What I Learned From a Game

I had built. The hoop was only about eight feet high, but that was better than nothing.

By the end of the season, after practicing on my own and playing with my team, I was still terrible; in fact, I hadn't made even one basket all season long.

In spite of how bad I was and that they had to let me play in every game, the Suns made it to the school's championship game. Guess who the team was that we had to play for the championship? You guessed it. We had to play my first team, the Blazers—the team that was so happy to get rid of me.

The game was close all the way through and I hadn't played at all. With only a few minutes left, my coach, who was an eighth grader, looked at my teammates and said, "Well, now I guess we lose the game. We have to let Neal play." The coach told me, "Neal, I want you to stay away from the ball and stay out of the way. If you stay out of the way, we might be able to win." With only a few seconds on the clock, my team was losing by one point. One of my teammates took a shot that missed. Even though I really wasn't part of the game, I was in the right place at the right time. The rebound fell into my hands. I threw the ball up underhanded and the ball went through the hoop as time ran out. That's right. The only basket the kid no one wanted on their team made all year long was the winning basket in the championship game. My teammates went nuts, cheering and hugging me.

Although I was still terrible, a strange thing happened that year. I fell in love with the game of basketball.

This leads me to ask the question: Which one of the players on my team was the most valuable player? Even though the other kids were better players, my team would not have won the

## What I Learned From a Game

championship if I had quit. Also, if the Blazers had not deliberately traded me, they might have won the championship game.

***The first lesson*** I learned from basketball was that regardless of a person's skill level, everyone can contribute as long as they never give up. If you really want something, never give up.

## *Everyone Is Special*

I continued to practice all the time. Little by little, I slowly got better. With all the practicing and hard work, by the time I was a senior in high school, I was not only one of the best players in the school, I was one of the best players in our league.

Every year, all the boys in the school had to play basketball in gym class. Each class picked teams and played against each other. In order to pick these teams, we needed captains. I was chosen to be one of the captains. As captain, I had to pick the players I wanted on my team.

Each captain took turns picking players from the class one at a time until everyone was picked. One of the players I picked was

# What I Learned From a Game

a boy named Bobby. Most of the kids in our school did not like Bobby. The other kids said he was dumb. He had no athletic abilities. Everyone in gym class told me he was going to be useless as a basketball player. I told them they were wrong, and I would prove it to them. I had no idea how Bobby was going to help my team. I just had a feeling that Bobby would make a difference.

Bobby had many natural talents, but sports wasn't one of them. It was very obvious Bobby hated sports and gym was the worst class he had to take. As we played our games, the other kids mocked Bobby. With all the mocking, Bobby wouldn't even try. Bobby walked up and down the court with his hands in his pockets. I told Bobby not to listen to the other kids. I told him to hang in there, and he would make a difference when it really counted.

After playing a number of games, my team was the best gym team in the school and was chosen to play against an all-star team. The all-star team was filled with players from my high school senior team. Everyone told me that there was no way we could beat such a good team, even if Bobby wasn't on our team. However, with Bobby as one of our players, we might as well not show up. I told them to watch and see.

The game was very close all the way through. Bobby just walked up and down the court the way he always did. After playing almost the entire game, the game was tied with only 26 seconds left on the clock. Guess who fouled out? That's right, I fouled out of the game and the other team had possession of the ball. They could run the clock down to the last few seconds before they had to shoot.

I called a time-out. All my teammates huddled around me except Bobby. I called him over and told my team this was Bobby's time. I told the other three players that I wanted them to play the

# What I Learned From a Game

best defense they had ever played. "Do not foul, and do not let them score."

I then told Bobby I wanted him to stand under our basket at the other end of the court and act like he wasn't part of the game. In other words, act the way he always did—standing with his hands in his pockets, showing no interest in the game.

I then told the other three players when the all-star team took their shot, I wanted all three of them to crash the boards, get the rebound, turn immediately, and throw the ball to Bobby. I told Bobby, "No one is going to be paying any attention to you. You will be wide open all by yourself. All you have to do is catch the ball and make a layup."

Well, that's exactly what happened: Bobby caught the ball and made a layup to win the game against the best players in the high school. As I said before, this all-star team was made up of players from my high school senior team. Just to let you know how good this all-star team was, our high school team won the league title that year and were ranked among the top teams in the state.

Bobby felt like a million dollars and the all-stars couldn't believe that Bobby, the boy everyone said was useless, beat them.

This brings us to the next question: Who was the most valuable player on my gym team? Was it me, the best player on our team who fouled out of the game? On the other hand, was it Bobby, the player who made the winning basket with me on the bench? You also have to consider the fact that the play I set up would not have worked if Bobby was not Bobby. We would not have won the game without him.

## What I Learned From a Game

*The second lesson* I learned from basketball was that you never know how valuable any one person may be. Never judge a person based on what they can't do. Always look for what they can do. Nurture a person's strengths, and you will be amazed at what they will contribute—not just to your life, but to other people's lives as well.

*Never underestimate anyone. Everyone is special.*

# You're the Second-Best Team

When I was a sophomore in high school, I was the sixth man on the school's junior varsity (JV) basketball team. For people who don't know anything about basketball, each team can have 12 active players. Out of these 12, each team is only allowed 5 players on the court at any given time. Being the sixth man meant there were five players who started the game (known as the Starting 5), and then I would be the first player off the bench to be inserted into the game. The remaining six players on the bench are considered the second team. The second team on my JV team primarily played when we were so far ahead in points that the game had already been won. In other words, the second team rarely, if ever, played when there was pressure to perform.

The first team of my sophomore JV team was a great team. We won most of our games by 15 to 20 points. In fact, we were so good that we beat our school's varsity team in a scrimmage. Oh,

# What I Learned From a Game

the varsity had a great deal of talent, but they didn't play as a team. Although my JV team didn't have as much talent as the varsity—after all, we were two years younger—we played as a team. The team that plays as a team can, and many times will, beat a more talented team where the players play as individuals.

As the season progressed, the JV team was undefeated, while the varsity team had a losing record. My JV coach was a great coach. The varsity coach was being embarrassed virtually every game; he was upset the JV team was always winning, and his varsity team was always losing. About three quarters of the way through the season, the varsity coach had enough of being embarrassed. He was going to do something about the JV team always winning, but what could he do? He began by taking our starting five and, one by one, moving them up to varsity.

We always had two games a week, one on Tuesday night and one on Friday night. Tuesday's game came and, as usual, we won and the varsity lost. Now we had to get ready for Friday's game. Friday's game was going to be against our archrivals, who were the second-best team in the league, just behind us. When I showed up to practice on Wednesday, I walked into the locker room to find only six other players. I asked, "Where is everybody else?" The six players there informed me that the coach of the varsity had taken the rest of our Starting 5 players and moved them up to varsity.

This meant there was only me, the sixth man, and the second team left. It was traditional for each team to have two captains. When the first team was taken away, our two captains were also taken. The other players were screaming and yelling, "We don't have a team anymore! Now we are going to be losers!"

# What I Learned From a Game

The first thing I had to do was to assess the situation. Not only did we have this gutted team that didn't have a captain, but, as I said before, we were going to be playing our archrivals in two days. We didn't even have enough players to scrimmage against one another! Our coach was a very positive man; however, when he walked into the locker room, we could see how crestfallen he was. He said, "Well, I guess the first thing we need to do is to vote for a captain." Although it was a long way from an enthusiastic atmosphere, the other players voted me as captain. After all, I had been the sixth man and was the only player left who had played when games were on the line.

After being named captain of this gutted team, I went to my coach to get his advice. My coach and I were pretty good friends. I really wanted his true feelings, so I spoke to him away from the other players. As we talked, he tried to be upbeat; however, he told me he didn't see any way we could beat our rival with the team we now had. I don't know why, but I have always been able to find something positive in negative or bad situations. When my coach told me we couldn't win, I told him that not only were we going to win, we were going to win by 20 points.

I then went back into the gym and told the other players we needed to work on our plays. We didn't even have enough players to practice against one another. However, we did have enough players to walk through our plays. I knew if we were going to win, we had to run our plays to perfection. When I told the other players to get up and start walking through the plays, they all just kind of looked at me. I asked them what the problem was. They just started shouting things like, "Why should we even try?" "We can't win!" "They are too good for us!" I literally started laughing. It was

## What I Learned From a Game

a genuine laughter. I was laughing so hard I almost fell down. My teammates just stared at me.

Through my laughter I asked them, "What's the best team you have ever played against?" They started shouting, "The team we are going to play on Friday!" I said, "WRONG! The best team you have ever played against was our first-string team. The team we had last night. The last time we played our rivals the first string beat them by 15 points. Every day in practice for this entire season, you guys not only have played against the best team in this league, but you held your own. Our rivals aren't even close to the team you have played every day for months. Our first team was the best team in this league by far. However, you guys are the second-best team in this league, bar none. Now get your butts out here and get ready to kick our rival's butts."

Two days later, on Friday night, we did just that. Not only did we win, we won by 20 points. You read that right, we won by five more points than our starting lineup had won by when they played our archrivals.

This brings us back to the question we have been asking throughout this book: Who's better? Was our first-string team really better than our second-string team? In contrast, was our second string the second string because they didn't believe they were as good as the first string? After all, the second string beat our archrivals by more points than our first string had.

***The third lesson*** I learned from basketball was that if you believe in yourself and the people around you, work hard and prepare, you can make it happen.

## What I Learned From a Game

# All Right, We Have The _____ Guy!

As time wore on, I became a fanatic about practicing and working out for basketball. I wore 20-pound weight jackets and ran up mountains. I pushed cars. I spent an hour every night sitting in front of the television stretching. I did anything I thought would increase my jumping ability.

One day, my best friend—who was black—and I were playing one-on-one. During our game, four black guys from out of town showed up. Neither my friend nor I had ever met any of these guys before. They watched us finish our game and then asked if we wanted to play three-on-three. We said, "Let's do it." We decided the best way to pick teams was to shoot foul shots. The first three who made their foul shots would be on one team. The other three would be on the other team. I went to the line and made my foul shot. Two of the black guys from out of town made their foul shots. That meant my team was two of the strangers and me. The other team was my black friend and the other two black strangers. Immediately after the two black strangers made their foul shots, they turned to one another and said, "ALL RIGHT, WE GOT THE WHITE GUY! HE CAN JUMP."

Now we have another question to ask: Who's the most valuable, the white player or the black player?

## What I Learned From a Game

*The fourth lesson* I learned from basketball was never to judge a person by the color of their skin. Skin color makes absolutely zero difference in what a person can contribute.

## *Everyone Is Welcome*

Throughout the years of playing basketball, I played a lot of pick-up games. Anyone who wanted to play just showed up at the courts and tried to get on a team. One of the things I noticed was the players who were picked for teams were picked for their ability to play. In other words, no one cared about anything except how good you were. If you could play and help their team win, then that's all that mattered.

There were black players, white players, Hispanic, and Asian players. There were female players of all races. No one asked whether you were Christian, Jewish, Muslim, or any other religion. Some of

# What I Learned From a Game

the females were openly gay. We had some young men show up who were also gay. However, when the teams were picked, no one cared about anything except whether they could help their team win.

So this brings us to another question: Who's the most valuable, the Hispanic, Asian, white, or black player? Is the girl, the Christian, the Jewish, or the Muslim person the most valuable player? Then again, maybe it's the gay player.

***The fifth lesson*** I learned from basketball was to never judge anyone by their gender, their religion, or their sexuality. Never judge a person by anything except the way they think, feel, and behave. In other words, only judge them by their inner character.

## What I Learned From a Game

---

# *The Results of These Experiences*

There are many other things basketball taught me. However, as far as *You're Amazing And I'll Prove It!* is showing us, these are the five most valuable things I learned:

1. Regardless of a person's skill level, everyone can contribute as long as they never give up. If you really want something, never give up.

2. You never know how valuable any one person may be. Never judge a person based on what they can't do. Always look for what they can do. Nurture a person's strengths, and you will be amazed at what they will contribute—not just to your life, but to other people's lives as well.

3. If you believe in yourself and the people around you, work hard and prepare, you can make it happen.

4. Never judge a person by the color of their skin. Skin color makes absolutely zero difference in what a person can contribute.

5. Never judge anyone by their gender, their religion, or their sexuality. Never judge a person by anything except the way they think, feel, and behave. In other words, only judge them by their inner character.

*If you start judging people by character and nothing else, you will be amazed at the overwhelming richness it will bring to your life.*

## What I Learned From a Game

> "I have a dream that my four little children will one day live in a nation where they will not be judged by the color of their skin but by the content of their character."
>
> *Martin Luther King Jr.[3] in his "I Have a Dream"[4] speech.*

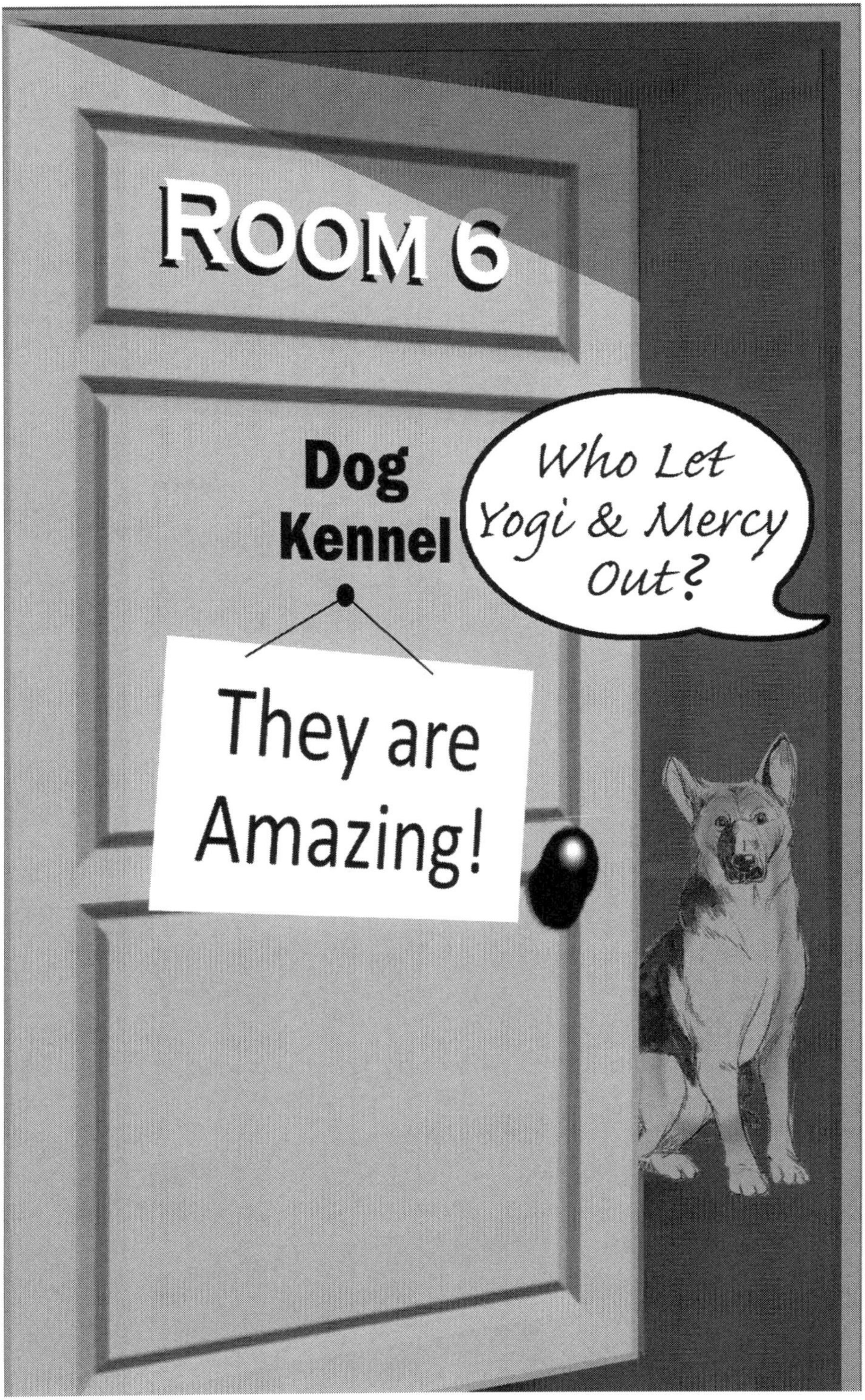
ROOM 6
Dog Kennel
Who Let Yogi & Mercy Out?
They are Amazing!

**Dog With The Wrinkled Face**

**Powerful, Athletic, Playful Dog**

In Room 2, we compared two incredibly different dogs. At the end of that section, I told you that later in this book, I would tell you two stories showing how remarkably special these breeds are. As I have told you, these two breeds (American Pit Bulls and Bloodhounds) are in a class called the "working dogs" class, and because they are so special, I had an exceptionally difficult time deciding which dog I should tell you about first. The way I finally decided was to flip a coin. Heads I would tell you about the Bloodhound first, and tails I would tell you about the American Pit Bull first. Just to let you know, I really mean I flipped a coin to decide. The coin landed tails up.

## Mercy, a Dog for You!

The answer to the question "Which dog is better?" came to me in two different ways. First, the dog on the right—the powerful, athletic, playful dog. My wife Linda and I had a Golden Retriever named Christmas. Christmas was a wonderful dog. However, one day he got very sick and died. Linda and I were both crying. Through my tears, I looked at Linda and said, "We have a choice; we can go home and cry, or we can honor Christmas by going to the SPCA (The Society for the Prevention of Cruelty to Animals)[5] and rescuing another dog."

At the SPCA, we were walking up and down the aisle looking at the different dogs. At one point, the director of the SPCA, a man by the name of Adam, told us there was a really nice dog he wanted to show us. Adam told us the SPCA had rescued this dog because her previous owners were abusing her. Adam told us the SPCA named this dog Mercy in honor of getting her away from her abusers. He then told us she was from a breed of dogs who had been given a bad name, which was undeserved.

Linda and I were skeptical, but we told Adam we would take a look at Mercy. However, Mercy didn't want anything to do with us. She was shy and timid. Mercy literally turned her back on us. Adam played with Mercy, but she still would not even look at Linda or me.

Adam explained that he and the other workers at the SPCA had fallen in love with Mercy, and that he and the other workers all took turns taking her home at night. He explained Mercy almost never spent the night at the SPCA. He said, "If you would just give Mercy a chance, you will never regret it. Just take her home for the weekend. If you don't love her by Monday, you can bring her back." Linda and I said, "OK, we will give Mercy until Monday." We took Mercy home on a Friday afternoon.

Well, it didn't take us until Monday to decide. We decided to keep her by Friday night. I have had many dogs in my life, but Mercy was the gentlest, best-behaved dog I have ever had. She didn't even run away when we opened the door. She just went out on the stoop and laid down. At this point, right at the beginning of our relationship with Mercy, I didn't understand how Mercy could be so different from her breed's reputation. I decided I would start researching the breed and find out all I could. The things I discovered astonished me.

I discovered they are actually known for being amazingly gentle, friendly, playful, and full of energy. Mercy's breed is known for being extremely strong, very fast, and absolutely tenacious—they simply will not give up. My research also taught me Mercy's breed is astonishingly loyal and completely fearless in the face of danger. They have one more extremely important trait: Mercy has an incredibly strong maternal instinct, which is the reason Mercy did not run away. I learned Mercy's maternal instinct is the reason her breed has been used for more than 100 years to watch over, play with, and protect children.

As I told you when we discussed the dogs earlier, Mercy's breed is the American Pit Bull. That's right, the exact breed of dog that we hear, on a daily basis, is so dangerous and ferocious. I discovered, both through personal experience and through research, that Pit Bulls are actually one of the gentlest, best-behaved breeds.

In my research on Pit Bulls, I found some amazing stories. One is about a Pit Bull named Sallie.[6] Sallie served in the 11th Pennsylvania Volunteer Infantry in the Civil War. Another story is about Sergeant Stubby,[7] who served in the 102nd Infantry assigned to the 26th Division in World War I. If you would like to see the awesome things Sallie and Sergeant Stubby did, you can go online and read about them.

## Yogi the Dog. Oh, So Special!

Now for the dog on the left. I have to admit that until fairly recently, I thought this dog was ugly and not particularly special.

It has wrinkly skin with lots of folds all over its face and neck. It has large, long floppy ears and slobbers all over itself. Before I knew better, these traits were ugly to me.

Then one day, this dog went from being ugly in my eyes to unbelievably special. You might ask, what changed my opinion so dramatically? The answer is a dog named Yogi.[8] I was watching a program on TV about a five-year-old little girl who had been taken from her home. The police searched for her for four days, but could not find a single clue. They then brought in Yogi the bloodhound to help find the little girl.

The police let Yogi smell a piece of the girl's clothing. After sniffing the clothing, Yogi turned and went out the door of the apartment. He went down the stairs and out into the parking lot. Yogi went across the parking lot and out onto the street. After several miles, Yogi made it to the interstate highway, went up the ramp, and started trotting down the side of the highway. As I am sure you know, there can be many miles between exits on interstate highways. However, that made no difference to Yogi. Yogi just kept trotting along the side of the highway, tracking the little girl.

Meanwhile Yogi's police handler was following him in his car. To save time and the dog's energy, Yogi's handler decided to pick Yogi up and drive him to the next exit ramp.

Once they arrived at the exit ramp, a number of miles down the highway, Yogi got out of the car. Yogi immediately picked up the girl's scent and trotted right past the exit. He again started trotting down the interstate toward the next exit.

Yogi's handler picked him up again and drove him to the next ramp. Once more, Yogi went past the ramp and headed down the interstate highway.

Yogi's handler repeated this action of picking him up and driving him to the next exit ramp. Finally Yogi, while sniffing for the girl's scent, trotted down a ramp and onto a town road.

Yogi trotted down the road for miles. At this point, Yogi's handler was concerned about the dog's health. This concern was because like the Pit Bull, Yogi's breed, the Bloodhound, is also known for being tenacious. Once you give them a job, they will not stop until they have finished it. This means Yogi would continue tracking the little girl until he was so exhausted he might die. For this reason, Yogi's handler decided to stop him and let him rest for the night.

The next day, Yogi's handler was going to bring him back to where he had left off. However, in the meantime, the police formed a search party and started looking for the little girl in the woods where Yogi had left off. The search party found the little girl in the woods less than two miles from where Yogi had led them.

If you think about what Yogi did, it is absolutely incredible. Not only was he able to follow the little girl's scent for miles and miles, but remember that the little girl had been riding in a car. Yogi was able to pick her scent up four days after she had been taken. Think about it: How much scent could she have possibly left after four days and miles and miles of her riding in a car?

As we said previously, Yogi's breed is a Bloodhound. After seeing this story, I decided I should do some research on Bloodhounds. I discovered that the very things that made Bloodhounds ugly to me—all the folds and wrinkly skin, along with their slobbering—were the very things that make them so special.

Like my research into Pit Bulls, my research into Bloodhounds also revealed some amazing stories. If you go online, you can find out much more about Bloodhounds than I am able to put in this book.

Although both of these breeds have extraordinary abilities, they also have weaknesses. One of the Bloodhound's weaknesses is directly due to their strength in picking up scents. You have to keep them fenced in, because if a Bloodhound picks up a scent that interests them, the dog will take off on their own. Once a Bloodhound picks up a scent, it is almost impossible to regain their attention.

One of the Pit Bull's weaknesses is their lack of ability to track scents. Like all dogs, the Pit Bull's sense of smell is much keener than that of humans. However, in comparison to the Bloodhound, their sense of smell is extremely weak. Another weakness comes directly from their enormous maternal instinct, which tells them they have a job to do. If you leave them alone for long periods of time, you have taken their job away, and they sometimes will tear something up in frustration.

You have already learned that the only thing that makes one person or thing better than another person or thing is only due to the needs you have in a specific situation. Now that you have all this new information about Bloodhounds and Pit Bulls, you can decide for yourself which dog you think is better: Yogi the Bloodhound, or Mercy the Pit Bull.

## Finding Your Natural Gift

Many of us don't know what our special gift to the world is. This special gift was given to us at birth. It is something that comes so naturally that many of us don't see it. Another word for this natural gift is our aptitude. One way to find our natural abilities is to take a simple aptitude test. However, from what I understand, most aptitude tests are questionnaires. These are simple pieces of paper with questions on it. They are not aptitude tests; they are "like" tests. These tests will show us what we may like to do, but it will not necessarily be our natural gift. Because of this, I don't recommend a "like" test. I recommend a test given by the Johnson O'Connor Research Foundation.

The Johnson O'Connor Research Foundation was founded in 1922. As of this writing, Johnson O'Connor has been studying and testing people's aptitudes for 95 years. Their test is a highly specialized test of hands-on puzzles and photos in which you actually use your natural gift. When I was a young man, I was interested in so many things that I had no idea of what I wanted to do for a living. When I heard about the aptitude test Johnson O'Connor was giving, I saved up my money and headed for the nearest city that had a Johnson O'Connor Research Foundation branch. In my case, the nearest branch was in New York City, but there are a total of 11 branches. After I took the test, they informed me I have the aptitude of an inventor/entrepreneur. I can't even begin to tell you how much this information has helped me. For more than 30 years, I have used the information I got from Johnson O'Connor to pursue my love of discovery.

The Johnson O'Connor Research Foundation literally saved me a lifetime of never knowing what I should be doing with my life. Because of this, if you are unsure of what you should be doing with your life, I highly recommend spending the time and money to take this test for yourself. It may literally save you a lifetime of frustration.

For more information, visit the Johnson O'Connor Research Foundation online at www.jocrf.org

# ROOM 7

**Real Life Continues**

Use What You've Learned to Decide

## A Little Girl Proves We Are All Special

Charlie, a friend of mine, told me an awesome story about his nine-year-old granddaughter. His granddaughter's name is Mere; the school Mere is in placed her in a special learning class because she has autism and is considered to be learning disabled. Charlie told me that at the time this story occurred, Mere was not even able to speak.

When Mere is at school, the teacher has time set aside for each student to do lessons on the computer. Well, Mere had other ideas. Instead of doing schoolwork, she wanted to watch something more entertaining: Disney princesses.

The teacher got Mere set up on the computer with her schoolwork. She then walked away, leaving Mere to do her work. A few moments later, the teacher looked over and Mere was watching Cinderella. She went over to Mere and said, "The computer in class is for schoolwork only." She turned off Cinderella and put Mere's schoolwork back on the screen. She said, "Do your schoolwork," and walked away. A few moments later, the teacher looked over and saw Snow White playing on the screen. Mere's teacher said, "I told you, you have to do your schoolwork. If you insist on watching cartoons, I will have to make it so you can't watch them."

Without Mere being able to see, the teacher went in and blocked the website she had been visiting with a password. The teacher then set up the schoolwork again, telling Mere, "Do your schoolwork." The teacher walked away, feeling as if she had fixed the problem.

The next time the teacher looked over, she was shocked because Mere had somehow hacked the password and was now watching Sleeping Beauty. Mere's teacher said, "You have got to be kidding me! How did you get past the security? OK, I will fix it." Mere's teacher put in a new, more complicated password. She then set Mere's schoolwork back up and told her, "Now, do your schoolwork."

The teacher walked away again. A little time passed and the teacher checked on her. This time when she looked at the screen, Mere was watching The Little Mermaid. Her teacher was dumbfounded and said, "I don't believe it. How could you have possibly hacked the password I just put in? That's it; you are going to do your schoolwork, young lady."

Mere's teacher went into the security screen for a third time. This time she put in an even more complicated password. Mere's teacher said, "There's no way you can get past this password." The teacher then set the schoolwork screen up for the fifth time, saying, "Now you have to do your schoolwork, young lady." As the teacher walked away, she must have been thinking, This little girl is supposed to be learning disabled. This is incredible. However, this time she has to do the work. The password I just put in is far too complicated.

This time Mere's teacher kept an eye on her just to make sure she was doing her work. It appeared the teacher had finally stumped Mere and she had to do her schoolwork. After some time of watching Mere out of the corner of her eye, the teacher turned her full attention back to the other kids in the class. The teacher

worked with the other kids for a while and then she went back to check on Mere. When she looked at the screen, Mere was doing her schoolwork. Well, if watching Beauty and the Beast is considered schoolwork. Mere had waited for the teacher to turn her attention to the other kids and then hacked the password for a third time.

## Who Is Better?

This brings us to the question we have been asking after we looked at all the other situations in this book: Who's better? Is it Mere or her teacher?

However, we also have to ask this question: If Mere is better, does that mean her teacher is somehow not as good? In contrast, if the teacher is better, then does that mean Mere is not as good?

So what do you think? Is Mere better than her teacher because she was able to hack into the computer and figure out the teacher's password? On the other hand, is Mere's teacher better? After all, the teacher is older with far more knowledge than Mere.

Before you make your decision on who's better, remember that at the time, Mere could not even speak. She is autistic and is considered to be learning disabled—but you must also remember Mere's teacher was having trouble finding a way to stop Mere from figuring out her password.

So who's better? As you ponder the answer, think back on everything you have seen and learned in this book. Think about all the different people and things we compared. Consider how your answer may or may not have changed when we placed them in specific situations. Think about how we compared the two trees. Take into account which tree you first thought was better. Remember how your opinion about which tree was better changed when we placed those same two trees in different situations.

Now, can you think of a scenario where Mere is better than the teacher? Next, I want you to think of a scenario where the teacher is better than Mere.

As you contemplate Mere and her teacher, let's jump back to the small ship and the big ship.

# Return to the Big Ship & the Small Ship

I told you we would talk about these two ships later in this book. Well, here we are! Let's compare them now.

*Small Ship With 3 Cannons* | *Big Ship With 30 Cannons*

In the final pictures of Room 1, I asked you to decide whether the small ship with 3 cannons is better than the big ship with 30 cannons. Then again, is the big ship with 30 cannons better than the small ship with 3 cannons?

When you first looked at the two ships, which one did you choose as being better than the other? I bet you picked the big, powerful ship.

However, now that you have read all the different stories in this book, do you think you should change your answer? Do you now think there is possibly a scenario where both ships could be in a position where each could have the upper hand?

Like all of the other comparisons you have made to this point, in order to answer the "who's better" question, we need to look at the capabilities as well as the limitations of the two ships.

At the beginning of the American Revolution, the Americans had no navy to speak of. England, on the other hand, had the most powerful navy in the world. England's navy ships were large, with lots of powerful cannons. When the Continental Congress decided to form America's first navy, they asked themselves how they would ever be able to compete against the world's largest and most powerful

***John Adams, Secretary of the Continental Navy***

ships. The Continental Congress responded by telling shipbuilders to make small, very fast ships. They knew there was no way America could compete head-to-head against such large, powerful ships. However, they could out-sail them. So in this case, England's larger, more powerful ships were better than America's smaller ships in size and power. But the smaller ships were better in speed and maneuverability.[9, 10]

With the small, fast ship strategy, America was able to capture

200 ships carrying supplies and other provisions to the English army. With these captured supplies, they were able to supply General George Washington[11] with desperately needed supplies. These supplies and provisions had a huge impact on America's ability to win their freedom.

So, in this case, the ship that is better depends on what you need it to do. The English man-of-war[12] ships were far better than America's small ships—in most aspects. However, the smaller, faster ships did exactly what America needed them to do: out-sail the English.

Does the strategy of smaller and faster against bigger and stronger sound familiar? Do you recall the Bald Eagle and the hummingbird? Mother Nature gave each bird its own specific strengths.

This tactic of using smaller and faster against larger and more powerful has been used successfully for thousands of years. In fact, if you watch a modern-day basketball game, you will see it used often with great success. One team will have big, very strong players against whom the other team cannot directly compete. So the team that can't compete head-to-head with strength will deliberately put a small, very fast team on the court. In many of these games, the smaller, faster team will win.

## What Do You Think Now?

This brings us back to Mere and her teacher. Have you decided if Mere has a place where she may be better than her teacher? In many ways, the large ship/small ship comparison is similar to the comparison I'm asking you to make about Mere and her teacher.

Mere's teacher, in many aspects, is better than Mere. However, Mere has such an extraordinary natural talent working with computers; in her own right, she has a place where she may be better than her teacher.

# I Want Chicken

Jim, another friend of mine, recently told me this incredible story about an event that happened to him when he was in college.

Jim told me he had always loved the chicken at the Jim Dandy restaurant. In his words, "It's the best chicken I've ever had." One day, while attending the American International College in Springfield, Massachusetts, he told his girlfriend about Jim Dandy's chicken. Jim told her there was a Jim Dandy restaurant not far from the college. He then told her he was going to go get some chicken. His girlfriend promptly informed him the restaurant was in the "black" part of town. She told him it was a very bad part of town. White people weren't allowed there. She said he should not go there.

Jim told her, "I want some Jim Dandy chicken. I'm going, and you should come with me." Jim's girlfriend was scared, but Jim was able to convince her to go with him.

Jim and his girlfriend jumped in their car and drove to the Jim Dandy restaurant. They parked, got out of the car, and headed for the restaurant. Jim's girlfriend was still scared. As they walked toward the restaurant, she was looking around for any trouble that may be lurking. Before they were able to get to the restaurant, a large, tough-looking black man stepped in front of the restaurant.

Jim's girlfriend turned and headed for the car.

Jim, on the other hand, just kept walking to the door. However, before he could get to the door, the black man stepped in front of him and said, "White people are not allowed here. You should leave NOW!"

Jim calmly looked at the black man and said,

"Do you know who Dr. Philip Blaiberg[13] is?" The black man in an angry voice said, "NO!" Jim said, "Dr. Philip Blaiberg was one of the first humans to ever have a heart transplant." The black man, still angry, said, "So what?" Jim continued, "Dr. Philip Blaiberg was white, and the heart he received was from a man named Clive Haupt. Clive Haupt was a black man who had died in an accident. Clive Haupt's heart was a match to Dr. Philip Blaiberg's. After the white-skinned Dr. Philip Blaiberg received the black-skinned Clive Haupt's heart he returned to full health. Dr. Philip Blaiberg was as active with Clive Haupt's heart as he had been with his own." Jim then pointed first to his white arm and then to the black man's arm as he said, "See? All this is, is pigmentation. Nothing more than decoration. On the inside, we are all the same."

The black man looked at Jim and said, "You are welcome here anytime."

Jim said, "That's great, but my girlfriend is scared to death of you. Would you do me a favor? Please walk over to her with me so she can meet you."

Jim and the black man walked over to Jim's girlfriend. Jim introduced her to him. They shook hands. Jim and his girlfriend then went into the restaurant and got chicken.

This true story is absolutely amazing and says it all.

**_Never judge a person by any physical characteristic. Only judge them by the way they think, feel, and behave. In other words, only judge them by their inner character._**

## Was There a Difference?

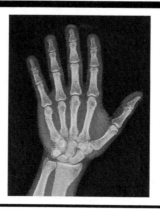

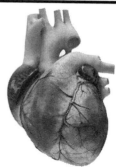

Now let's return to the skeletal hands, the brains, and the hearts. Regardless of whether you think all the photos are the same or not, I want you to take a moment to look at them again. On the next few pages, you will find the same pictures you looked at earlier in this book. Only this time, instead of three pictures of each to compare, you will notice I have added a fourth skeletal hand, brain, and heart. Hopefully, the fourth picture will make it easier for you to compare them.

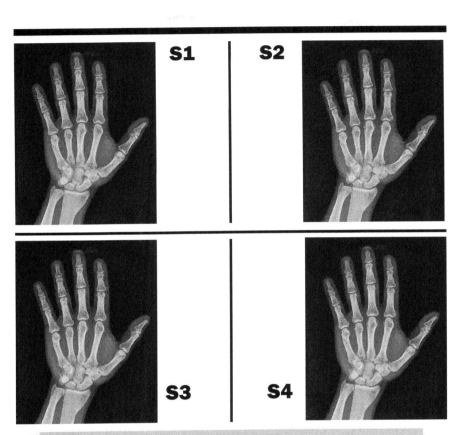

Don't spend a lot of time, but take a moment to examine the skeletal hands just like you did before. Only this time, when you compare them, I want you to reflect back on the five things we learned from basketball. (If you need to refresh your memory, look back at Room 5, page 80, "The Results of These Experiences"). With these five things in mind, can you tell me if these four skeletal hands are the same or not?

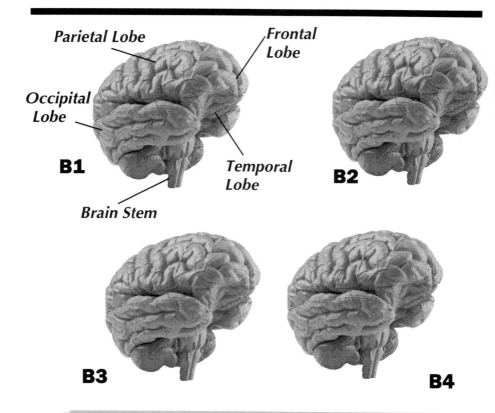

*Parietal Lobe*

*Frontal Lobe*

*Occipital Lobe*

**B1**

*Temporal Lobe*

**B2**

*Brain Stem*

**B3**

**B4**

As you look again at these brains, keep in mind the stories you read about the black doctor, the Asian lawyer, and the white short person. While keeping these stories in mind, can you tell me if these brains are all the same?

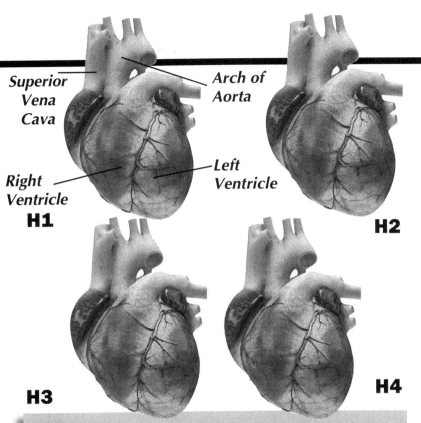

Superior Vena Cava

Arch of Aorta

Right Ventricle

Left Ventricle

**H1**

**H2**

**H3**

**H4**

When you first looked at the hearts, did you think they are all the same, or are there some differences? Regardless of your answer, I want you to take another look. However, this time, when you evaluate them, I want you to take into consideration all the stories and comparisons you have read about in this book. As you look at these hearts, pay close attention to the story my friend Jim told about the black man he met outside the chicken restaurant. Keeping all this in mind, can you now tell me, are the hearts all the same?

While you looked at the skeletal hands, brains, and hearts, did you keep in mind the stories I told you to remember? If you did, then you probably said the answer to the question "Are they all the same?" is "Yes, they are all the same."

In order for you to find the differences, you have to look at the owner of each skeletal hand, brain, and heart. The skeletal hand of the black doctor is identical to the Asian lawyer and the white short person. The same is true for the brains and the hearts.

I also wonder if you noticed I never told you whether the doctor, the lawyer, or the short person were men or women. I didn't tell you whether any of them were Jewish, Christian, Muslim, or any other faith. I didn't tell you their eye color or their hair color. Nothing was said about whether they are heavy or thin. I never told you how old they are. I also didn't tell you their sexual preferences. I only told you what their skin color or ethnicity was.

Now that you know that their skin color or ethnicity makes no difference whatsoever, do you think it makes any difference whether any one of these three people is male or female? Does it make any difference whether they are Jewish, Christian, Muslim, or any other faith? If you needed legal help, would it matter that the lawyer is 70 years old? If you needed the expertise of the doctor, would it make any difference whether they are straight or gay? If you were lost in the wilderness, would you care if the short person was a 15-year-old girl? OF COURSE NOT! If you need legal help, you need a lawyer; if you need medical help, you need a doctor; and if you are lost in the wilderness, you need someone who knows how to survive.

As my friend Jim explained to the black man outside the chicken restaurant, we are all the same on the inside; nothing else matters.

You might be asking, "What about the fourth skeletal hand, brain, and heart? Who do they belong to?"

Who do you think they belong to? Do they belong to the captain of the basketball team (me)? Then again, they might belong to Bobby, the player who made the winning basket against the all-star team. You might think they belong to Mere, the little girl who hacked past her teacher's computer password. Possibly they belong to my friend Jim, or the black man with whom he spoke.

You may also be asking whether the fourth set of organs is exactly the same as those of the doctor, the lawyer, and the short person. The answer to this question is yes. The fourth skeletal hand, brain, and heart are exactly the same as the other three sets. And the person they belong to is YOU!

# ROOM 8

## What This Book Is All About

A Lifetime of Freedom!

## Open-Minded Knowledge Is Freedom

"When we allow freedom to ring—when we let it ring from every city and every hamlet, from every state and every city, we will be able to speed up that day when all ... children, black men and white men, Jews and Gentiles, Protestants and Catholics, will be able to join hands and sing ... 'Free at last, Free at last, ... we are free at last.'"

*Martin Luther King Jr. in his "I Have a Dream" speech.*

Before reading this book, you already knew we are all physically different on the outside. However, you now know we are all the same on the inside. You also now know we all have abilities that make each and every one of us uniquely special in our own ways.

You have learned our unique abilities make each of us better than others in some situations, and not as good in others. The situations where your knowledge and/or skills make you better than others do not make you superior to the others around you—they just put you in a leadership position. The situations where your knowledge and/or your skills put you in the lesser position do not mean you are inferior to the people around you—they just mean you are in a follower position.

When I started writing this book, I didn't know myself what it was about. Up until now, I have not told you what it is about. I didn't tell you because it would have influenced you. This influence could have changed your answers to the questions you have answered to this point.

The last experience I had before I started writing this book was the encounter with the spiders in the bright room and the dark room. Do you remember the spiders I asked you to compare in the fifth set of drawings in Room 1, "Let's Compare," and Room 2, "Does It Make a Difference"? After I had this experience with the spiders, a little voice inside me told me to start writing this book.

At that time, I thought it was nuts to write a book about a big spider and a small spider. However, something inside of me wanted me to write, so I started writing. When I started writing, I thought this book was about spiders and trees in different situations. It wasn't until I had written up to the point of my friend Jim and his encounter with the black man that I realized this book is about acceptance of not only the people around you, but also acceptance of yourself. Once you have seen and accepted how special you are, you can then accept the people around you. With this acceptance, you then eliminate narrow-mindedness. Some people call it "bigotry." I gave you the definition of "acceptance" and "bigotry," along with several other words, at the end of Room 4 under the heading "What Have We Learned From These Stories?" Do you remember what these words mean? Just to refresh your memory I have listed the Merriam-Webster Dictionary definitions again below:

**Accept** is "to receive willingly; to give admittance or approval; to recognize as true; to make a favorable response to."

**Special** is "being unusual and especially better in some way; different from others of the same kind—unique; designed for a certain purpose."

**Bigotry** is "intolerance."

A **bigot** is "one who is strongly partial to one's own group, religion, race, or politics and is intolerant of those who differ."

An **intolerant** person is "not willing to allow some people to have equality, freedom, or other social rights."

**Narrow-minded** is when a person is "not willing to accept opinions, beliefs, or behaviors that are unusual or different from their own."

Once I realized this book was about these words, and keeping the dictionary's definitions in mind, I asked myself two questions.

*Question one: What do I know, and how do I know anything about narrow-minded intolerance?*

At the time of writing this book, I am 58 years old. I am so far removed from my youth, I honestly had not thought about my first 11 years of life for more than 40 years. I was then put in a situation where I had to go back and not only think about my first 11 years of life of dealing with narrow-minded intolerance, but I had to experience those days again. This experience was excruciatingly difficult. However, something inside of me was telling me I had to revisit my youth in order to write the last part of this book.

So, to state the question more completely, how do I, Neal G. Brownell, a white man, know anything about narrow-minded intolerance? Here is my story of how I learned the things I am teaching in this book.

# Only Narrow-Minded Intolerance for a Little Blind Boy

*In order to teach something, a teacher needs to have knowledge of the subject. The more intimate the knowledge, the more information a teacher can pass on to the student.*

I was born into a family with five older siblings, all of them straight "A" students. However, when I, little Neal, came along, it was a different story. To my parents and siblings, I was mentally slow, and I was most definitely very clumsy. In fact, I was so clumsy that I spent two years of the first four years of my life without a toenail on either one of my big toes. I was always stubbing my toes or dropping something on them. When it was time for me to read, I couldn't do it. Heck, I couldn't even catch a ball.

My parents took me to see a specialist. The specialist diagnosed me as "retarded." Nowadays we would say I was "mentally challenged." However, I did not experience this kind way of saying it. My experience was of people being harsh, narrow-minded, and intolerant.

My parents were thoroughly embarrassed. How could they have five book geniuses and then have me? What would they tell their friends and neighbors?

My parents were able to hide me (little Neal) until I started first grade. But in first grade, I was actually required to learn something. I not only didn't learn anything, I wouldn't even accept what the teacher was teaching. I was always asking questions and saying things like "I don't believe you."

My teacher became so angry with me that she actually told my mother I was a waste of time. She said, "I'm not going to waste one minute trying to teach him." Needless to say, I failed first grade.

Before I started first grade for the second time, someone suggested that my parents have my eyes checked. The eye doctor informed them that I was virtually blind.

At this point, you would think my parents would have been elated. "Little Neal's not mentally slow! He's blind!" But no, not my parents. They were horrified. They said, "Oh no, you're not only mentally slow, but you're also blind."

For most people, home is a sanctuary. A place they can get away from narrow-minded intolerance. But not for me. Day after day, year after year, my parents told me I was stupid. My siblings let me know I was dumb and inferior. The kids at school used to say, "Here comes the dummy!" and even the teachers judged me with the same narrow-mindedness.

I passed first grade the second time because I was too old to hold back. I somehow made it through second grade, but failed third grade. The only reason I made it to fifth grade was because the school said I was too old to keep holding back.

***I know all of this sounds terrible, but the world works in extremely strange ways. I was about to learn how to accept myself as unique and special.***

When I started fifth grade, my parents sent me to a school for kids like me. There I met the first person who believed in me: Mrs. Anderson.

Mrs. Anderson did two extraordinary and yet unbelievably simple things. First, she realized I was an extremely inquisitive little boy. I did not want to be told something was true, I wanted to be shown. The second thing she did was tell me I was smart. I was just a little boy, but I looked at her and said, "NO, I'm stupid." She looked me straight in the eye and said, "You're smart, and I'll prove it to you." Mrs. Anderson then set out to have me do one assignment after another that I was able to do. After each assignment, she said, "See? I told you that you are smart, and this proves it."

At the end of fifth grade, the next major change in my life took place. It's a change I would not have chosen, but somehow things really do work out for the best. The change that happened was Mrs. Anderson was taken away from me. My family moved from a big-city school in Philadelphia to a small-town school in Millbrook, New York.

At my new school, no one knew me as the dummy. All they saw was the smart little boy Mrs. Anderson had unveiled. The narrow-minded intolerance at home continued for many years, and to some degree, it still exists today. But after Mrs. Anderson taught me I was smart, I no longer listened to my parents and siblings.

Many amazing things came out of my story; however, there are three main things.

**First,** rather than look at me with the narrow-minded intolerance my family and the other people around me did, Mrs. Anderson accepted me and was the first person to look deeper. She saw that I was an inventor. Inventors are so inquisitive, they want to know every detail about the subject they're studying. They ask so many silly questions that most people, when hearing the questions think, "There must be something wrong with this guy."

---

The second and third things that came out of my experience of having to deal with this narrow-minded intolerance are far more important.

**The second thing** Mrs. Anderson taught me is that all it takes is one person to accept and believe in someone to completely change their life forever. I strive to be that person with everyone I meet.

**The third thing** that came out of my experience came because I spent the first six years of my life being virtually blind. I had the rare privilege to get to know people by sensing their spirits rather than seeing their physical forms. I carry this ability of knowing who someone is on the inside with me to this very day. Because of this ability, I have a hard time understanding bigotry.

Although I—like everyone else, at times—have been guilty of judging people by some characteristics, as far as physical characteristics go, I don't see black and white, young or old, male or female, or any other physical characteristic. I see how special the person in front of me is. I absolutely love the differences between our religions, our cultures, between men and women, between the races, between young and old, or any other difference you can find.

*We need to celebrate our differences. This is also called our "diversity," which encompasses all of our differences. It's what makes us so special.*

For the reasons I've outlined in the above writing, I believe I went through these experiences so I could write this book about acceptance, as well as narrow-minded intolerance. As you can see, I know the subject extremely well. I believe I'm supposed to show people how liberating acceptance is, as well as how stupid, limiting, and narrow-minded bigotry is. I also believe I'm supposed to show you not only how special other people are, but how special you are.

**You were made just the way you are for a reason. Many times, you will not know what that reason is for quite some time. So hang in there. When the time is right, you will be shown what your special gifts are.**

I told you earlier in this book that I too have been guilty of judging some things and some people from a narrow-minded point of view. So when I speak of bigotry, please don't think I am pointing any fingers. I am not talking down to anyone or any group. We have all been guilty of narrow-minded biases in our lives. This most definitely includes me.

As I said earlier in this section, once I realized this book was about acceptance as well as narrow-minded intolerance, and keeping the dictionary's definition in mind, I asked myself two questions.

We just explored the answer to question one, which was, "What do I know, and how do I know anything about narrow-minded intolerance?"

Now for the second question.

---

*Q*uestion two: *If I had to describe what narrow-minded intolerance or bigotry is in my own words, would I describe it the same as the dictionary?*

I am a person who asks questions all the time. When I ask myself questions, they usually lead me to more questions. Bigotry is not as simple and cut-and-dried as the dictionary says. My personal definition for bigotry is far more detailed.

## My Definition of Narrow-Minded Bigotry

Throughout this book, you have looked at different situations and answered question after question. You have opened your mind and looked at many things from different angles. Many were angles you probably never considered before. What you have done with this book is the polar opposite of bigotry.

Being narrow-minded is not disagreeing with someone. It is closing your mind to any point of view that may differ from the one you already hold. It is also pre-judging everyone who has the same characteristics as being bad, and refusing to change your mind about them regardless of the situation. As you have seen, this intolerance can be aimed at anyone or anything. It is OK to disagree with someone if your disagreement comes from gaining as much knowledge as possible. Bigotry hurts everyone involved. However, it hurts the closed-minded person the most. Can you imagine what would happen to a person who formed an opinion based on narrow-mindedness?

Think back to Room 4 in this book. Do you remember the story of the plane crash? What do you think would have happened to you if you made your decision based on bigotry? You would not have survived! Now I ask you, who would've been hurt the most by your narrow-minded decision?

So, my definition of bigotry is when a person forms an opinion on extremely narrow parameters. Once the opinion is formed, they close their mind to anything or anyone that offers additional factual information that is in opposition to their opinion.

A bigoted decision is made with limited or skewed knowledge at best, and out-and-out false knowledge at worst. Because the person being narrow-minded thinks the decision was made with knowledge, they actually believe it is reasonable and logical. After forming the decision, a person being closed-minded refuses to consider any other factual information presented to them.

That's the nice definition. Another definition of bigotry is when a person forms an opinion out of fear, which oftentimes leads to hate. They may think a person is going to take their job, and they will not be able to survive. They may also believe a country, or a political party, wishes harm to them personally. This fear leads the intolerant person to act with unreasonable hatred at best, complete evil at worst. The fear that the closed-minded person formed the opinion on was also formed from limited, skewed, or false information. Because the person being closed-minded believes their decision is based on truth and knowledge, they steadfastly stand by the decision, refusing to see any scenario that may force a re-examination of their position.

As you can see, my definition is much more detailed than

the dictionary definition. The dictionary definitions for bigotry and narrow-minded intolerance are so narrow that they make bigotry sound like it's easily understood. It makes it sound like it's just about people and/or their opinions concerning one another. Bigotry is so much deeper than this. It can literally manifest itself in almost every aspect of life. You can be intolerant of seeing another point of view concerning not just people, but objects, like the big and small ship. You can have narrow-minded views about a country. You can literally have narrow-minded views about _____ itself. (I deliberately didn't fill in the blank in order to make a point.)
Let's look at some scenarios that illustrate this idea.

# Person 1: Who Am I?

■ My home is dirty and it is poorly ventilated. In fact, the ventilation is so poor, that smoke often backs up into the house.
■ I have no electricity, or anything that electricity runs:
- •No electric lights
- •No radio
- •No television
- •No refrigerator
- •No fans
- •No air conditioning
- •No central heating
- •No running water on demand
- •No computer
- •Or anything else you can think of

- I have no video cameras or any accessories that go with the cameras.
- My telephone is so limited and unreliable, you might as well say I don't have one.
- I have limited access to food.
- The cars I have access to are extremely unreliable. In fact, they are so unreliable, they are out-and-out dangerous.
- My home is heated with a fireplace or a coal stove, with no other means of heating it.
- I have no modern plumbing.
- It's extremely difficult for me to travel long distances from my home.
- My access to health care is so limited that you might as well say I have none.

**Who am I and where do I live?**

# Person 2: Who Am I?

- I own and live on my own beautiful property.
- I have electricity and everything that goes with it:
  - Electric lights
  - Radio
  - Television
  - Refrigerator
  - Fans
  - Air conditioning

- •Central heating
- •Running water on demand
- •I have three computers, multiple printers, scanners, and lots of other equipment
- ■ As well as a myriad of other things that run on electricity. I have three $5,000 video cameras and $10,000–$15,000 of accessories that go with the cameras.
- ■ I have three of the best telephones money can buy.
- ■ I have access to all the food I can eat and it's the largest variety of food known to man. I literally have access to food from anywhere in the world, year-round, and at any time of day.
- ■ All my vehicles are safe and reliable.
- ■ My home is centrally heated with oil and I have a beautiful wood stove.
- ■ I have indoor plumbing.
- ■ I can travel anywhere in the world at a moment's notice.
- ■ I have access to extraordinarily good health care.

## Who am I and where do I live?

You probably don't know these two people personally. However, you should at least know of these two people.

## *Have you guessed who these two people are?*

I will let you think about this question while we look at some other situations.

# My Own Bigotry

A s I said earlier, we all have been guilty of not accepting some one or some things and judging them with narrow-minded intolerance, and I am no exception to the rule. The fact is, any time you judge a person or a thing on very narrow parameters, you are being narrow-minded. Earlier in this book, I told you how I was narrow-minded regarding Pit Bulls and Bloodhounds before I learned of their special attributes.

Sometimes we put blinders on and don't look at the whole picture before we make a decision. This is something we need to work on every day. When we don't see the whole picture, we can't let these special people or things help us.

Case in point: My first wife, Deb, who died, had a brother and a cousin who used to drive me nuts. I have to admit I really didn't like either of them. My brother-in-law used to do really dumb things and then tell everyone how funny he thought they were. My wife's cousin used to take charge and force other people to do things her way. I always saw these things as negatives until my wife was in the hospital on her deathbed.

Deb was only 38 years old. She was a healthy woman in the morning, and that night she was in the hospital. She had gone to work and collapsed on the floor. They rushed her to the hospital, ran some tests, and then took her to surgery. The surgery was supposed to take around six hours.

As you can imagine, this was a terrible time for all of us. Six hours is an eternity when you are waiting for a loved one in a life-or-death surgery. During this time, my brother-in-law was in the waiting room with the rest of our family and friends. For the entire time, he told one story after another of his escapades—the ones I used to think were so annoying. Everyone, including me, sat around laughing the entire time. The six hours flew by.

When the doctors finally came into the waiting room, the news was not good. The doctor who spoke told us Deb would probably never wake up. The next day, she died. I was devastated. We had known each other since we were in sixth grade. I was in shock. There was so much to do and in my condition there was no way I could do it. Then my wife's cousin came to me and asked if she could handle some of the things that needed to be done. I told her I would greatly appreciate anything she could help me with. The first thing she did was grab a piece of paper and start making her way around the room. She asked everyone there to tell her stories about my wife. She later used these stories to write my wife's obituary.

What I learned from this story was that the very things I didn't like about my brother-in-law and my wife's cousin were the very things I needed when it really mattered. My brother-in-law lightened everyone's burden during one of the most trying times of my life. My wife's cousin's take-control attitude was exactly what I needed in the aftermath of my wife's death.

Since Deb's death, I have been extremely thankful for my brother-in-law and my wife's cousin being just the way they are.

**Always try to see the good in what you perceive as someone's shortcomings. They may be exactly what you need when things are at their worst.**

Are you still thinking about my statement? I said, "You can literally have narrow-minded views about _____ itself." Have you figured out what should go in the blank? I will give you a hint. The two people I introduced you to (Person 1 and Person 2) have everything to do with what goes in the blank.

## Have You Guessed Who Person 1 & Person 2 Are?

As I said before, you probably don't know Person 1 and Person 2 personally. However, you should at least know of these two people. If you have not guessed who they are, let me give you some more information about each of them.

One of these people has servants to help them with their life. The other does not. One of these people not only lives in a mansion, but has multiple mansions. The other lives in a trailer that's almost 30 years old.

One gives orders, and people all over the world carry them out. The other not only does not give orders, but no one would listen if they did. With the finest medical assistance money can buy, one of these people has any medicine they need to ensure they are in the best health. With no way of acquiring modern medical help, one of these people has suffered with cataracts and long periods of devastating depression. One of these people is obviously rich, while the other is obviously very poor.

I want you to look at each of these circumstances and decide which person they belong to. Just look at the descriptions listed below and circle which person each one belongs to. If you think the item goes with Person 1 described earlier in this room, circle

1st person. If it goes with Person 2, circle 2nd person. In order to answer these questions, quickly refer back to the descriptions of Person 1 and Person 2 on pages 121 - 123.

1. Has servants to help: 1st person or 2nd person
2. Has no servants: 1st person or 2nd person
3. Lives in multiple mansions: 1st person or 2nd person
4. Lives in a trailer that's almost 30 years old: 1st person or 2nd person
5. Gives orders, and people all over the world carry them out: 1st person or 2nd person
6. Has devastating depression along with cataracts, with no way of acquiring modern medical help: 1st person or 2nd person
7. Has people—not servants—who will do a myriad of things for them: 1st person or 2nd person

Now that you have made your decision as to which of the seven items goes with which person, let's see if your answers are right.

1. Has servants to help: the 1st person.
2. Has no servants: the 2nd person.
3. Lives in multiple mansions: the 1st person.
4. Lives in a trailer that's almost 30 years old: the 2nd person.
5. Gives orders, and people all over the world carry them out: the 1st person.
6. Has devastating depression along with cataracts, with no way of acquiring modern medical help: the 1st person.
7. Has people—not servants—who will do a myriad of things for them: the 1st and the 2nd person.

You may be asking why the answer to Question 7 should be "both people." As you will see when I introduce you to these people, each of them has access to people who are not servants. These people who are not servants will do things for these two people just because they ask them for their help.

I bet you got most of them wrong. But how can that be? Do you remember earlier, in this Room, when I wrote this? You can literally have narrow-minded views about _____ itself. I don't know what you thought the blank should be filled in with, but the correct answer is TIME. That is right. If we do not educate ourselves, we can form an opinion that is based on such limited knowledge that we can actually be biased toward the very time in which we live.

The fact is, the first person listed above is Queen Victoria.[14] She was Queen of England from 1837 to 1901. Queen Victoria was arguably the most powerful person ever to live. She reigned over more land on earth than anyone in history. Yet, the second person lives a better life than she did.

Who is the second person? The second person is Neal G. Brownell. In other words, me. At the writing of this book, in comparison to many people in America, I have almost nothing. However, I have so much that I literally live better than Queen Victoria did. A number of years ago, I decided I would make decisions for my life based on what I really needed, and not what would impress the neighbors. This simplified my life to the point that I have an incredibly good life full of abundance and joy with very little stress.

All of us really need to take a good look at our lives. We need to realize how incredible our lives are. Depending on our own decision-making, we can live lives that are relatively stress-free and full of more abundance than kings and queens had not that long ago.

Think about this for a moment: The average person in this country lives a far better life than all the kings in all of history prior to 1970. As of this writing, we are comparing your life with kings who lived only 45 years ago.

In 1970, kings did not have:

- The cars we have today
- The computers we have today
- The phones we have today
- The televisions we have today
- The medicine we have today
- The medical advancements we have today
- The list goes on

Don't get me wrong—I am not saying our lives are easy and without any stress. What I am saying is, we live in the easiest time in history to live. I was at a party with a lot of mothers and fathers who have young kids. I told them I thought today is the easiest time in history to raise kids. At the time, I had two young kids. You would think I just shouted "Fire!" in a packed theater. The parents at the party started shouting and yelling at me. "Are you out of your mind?" "You have to be nuts!" "What is wrong with you?" I put my hands up to calm them down and then said, "You didn't listen to what I just said. I didn't say it is easy to raise kids today. I know it's a monumental task. However, I believe today is the easiest time in history to raise kids."

Up until very recently, if parents had a problem with their children, they were on their own. There was no one to help them. However, nowadays it doesn't matter what your problem is—help is only a phone call or a click away. So I am not saying today is an easy time in which to live. What I am saying is, because of the many resources at our fingertips, today is the easiest time in history to live.

### *Our lives are amazing and if you make someone else's life better, you can make your own life extraordinary!*

# ROOM 9

**Just the Beginning**

Your Exceptional Life Starts Now!

You may be asking yourself how you can prevent yourself from becoming closed-minded. Or, if you've noticed that you have become (or have a tendency to be) closed-minded, how can you change that about yourself? The easiest way to avoid being closed-minded is to question everything. Never accept anything at face value. Just because someone tells you something is true does not make it true. Once you form your opinion, be open-minded enough to at least consider a different point of view. The different point of view may change your mind, and it may not. However, just by looking at your formed opinion from a different angle, you are growing in knowledge. **KNOWLEDGE IS POWER!**

## "Question with boldness..."
*Thomas Jefferson*[15]
*Third President of the*
*United States of America*

**Keep an open mind. Treat others with kindness and understanding. Accept others for who they are. Always keep a sense of humor. Find something funny in everything. Stand on your own two feet, and your life will be extraordinary.**

I have been blessed with a life that has brought me into contact with amazing men and women of all ages, races, and backgrounds.

I also have been in situations where people told me who someone else was before I met them. I was told one person was just a crazy old farmer. Another person was described as mentally slow, and another person was just a dumb woman working as a cashier. After I had the privilege to meet these people, I realized that the people telling me who they were only looked at them with extremely shallow eyes. They were looking at the physical characteristics and

at their limitations, rather than looking at the astonishing things these individuals could do. After getting to know these three extraordinary people, I am proud to say they are all my friends. I am pleased to say I have asked them, as well as many other supposedly unremarkable people, to use their exceptional gifts to help me from time to time. I am humbled to say they have also asked me to help them.

My life has taught me that there is no person who is inferior or superior at all times. Regardless of age, race, gender, sexual orientation, religion, or any other differences, each and every one of us is a **GENIUS** in at least one thing. Our job is to find this special gift, both in ourselves and others, cultivate it, and help each other to help each other.

So the next time you meet someone, rather than looking at their differences as weaknesses, look at them as amazing strengths. Ask yourself: "Who is this person?" and "What are the unique gifts they bring to the world?"

Remember that earlier in this book I told you that you are an

---

exceptionally special person? I also told you that if you didn't already know you are exceptionally special, I would prove it to you.

Most people only look at what's presented to them. The average person also only looks at things the way other people tell them to look at them. It takes an amazing person to look at a situation and see it through their own eyes.

This is what you have done in this book. You have looked at situations from different angles and come up with your own opinions. It takes a remarkable person to stand on their own two feet, to assess what's in front of them and make up their own mind. This is why I told you earlier that you are an exceptional person—the average person wouldn't have made it this far in this book. I knew you were exceptional, and now you know it too.

Now go and make your life, as well as the lives of people around you, **EXTRAORDINARY!**

# Endnotes

## Room 2 – Does It Make a Difference?

1. Your Purebred Puppy, "Bloodhound Temperament: What's Good About 'Em, What's Bad About 'Em," accessed March 2016.
   *www.yourpurebredpuppy.com/reviews/bloodhounds.html*

2. Jake Flanagin, "The Tragedy of America's Dog: A brief history of the vilification of the Pit Bull," Pacific Standard, 28 February 2014, accessed February 2016.
   *www.psmag.com/nature-and-technology/
   tragedy-americas-dog-pit-bull*

## Room 5 – Real Life

3. Biography, "Martin Luther King Jr.," accessed 23 March 2017.
   *http://www.biography.com/people/
   martin-luther-king-jr-9365086#synopsis*

4. Martin Luther King Jr., U.S. Government Archives, "I Have a Dream Speech," accessed 23 March 2017.
   *https://www.archives.gov/files/press/exhibits/dream-
   speech.pdf*

## Room 6 – Who Let Yogi & Mercy Out?

5. The Society for the Prevention of Cruelty to Animals, accessed 23 March 2017.
   *https://www.aspca.org*

6. The State of New York and the Civil War, "Sallie, Mascot of the 11th PA Vol. Infantry," accessed 23 March 2017.
   *www.nycivilwar.us/sallie.html*

7. Smithsonian National Museum of American History, The Price of Freedom: Americans at War, "Stubby," accessed 23

# Endnotes

---

March 2017.
*amhistory.si.edu/militaryhistory/collection/object.asp?ID=15*

8. Unsolved: More Mysteries, "Alie Berrelez," accessed 23 March 2017.
*http://unsolved.com/archives/alie-berrelez*

## Room 7 – Real Life Continues

9. Charles Brodine, "A Look at the Birth of the Continental Navy," America's Navy, 21 October 2009, accessed March 2016.
*www.navy.mil/submit/display.asp?story_id=49113*

10. Tim McGrath, Give Me A Fast Ship. New York (Penguin Group), 2014.

11. Biography, "George Washington," accessed 23 March 2017.
*www.biography.com/people/george-washington-9524786*

12. Some Interesting Facts, "Man of War Ship," accessed 23 March 2017.
*www.someinterestingfacts.net/man-of-war-ship/*

13. Bionity, "Philip Blaiberg," accessed 23 March 2017.
*www.bionity.com/en/encyclopedia/Philip_Blaiberg.html*

## Room 8 – What This Book is All About

14. History Today, "Pioneering Royals," accessed 23 March 2017.
*www.historytoday.com/blog/2012/06/pioneering-royals*

## Room 9 – Just the Beginning: Your Exceptional Life Starts Now!

15. Brainy Quote, Thomas Jefferson accessed 28 April 2017.
*www.brainyquote.com/quotes/quotes/t/thomasjeff141347.html*

# Photo Credits

Pages 55, 102, 103 Skeletal Hand - istockphoto.com
Pages 56, 102, 104 Brain - istockphoto.com
Pages 57, 102, 105 Heart - istockphoto.com

## About the Author

Neal G. Brownell is the inventor of "The Bandit™," a basketball shooting accuracy trainer that puts your arm in the proper shooting position every time. For ten years he and his first wife Debra ran Brownell Enterprises, selling The Bandit™ and a number of programs he wrote to coach kids interested in playing basketball. These programs include Laser Shot™ (a shooting and rebounding program), Skybound™ (this program helps improve on your jumping ability and your all-around game) and Mental Power™ (you must be mentally prepared to win) to name a few. If you would like to obtain "The Bandit™" or any of these programs for the young basketball star in your life, please send an e-mail to nealgbrownell@gmail.com. He has also coached basketball on an individual basis.

Neal loves helping people to better their lives. He currently lives in the Catskills with second wife, Linda and their two Pit Bull mixes: Mercy and Mr. Brown.

Made in the USA
Middletown, DE
28 December 2018